EMMANUEL JOSEPH

The Curious Solitary, How Resilience and Nostalgia Shape Our Inner Worlds

Copyright © 2025 by Emmanuel Joseph

All rights reserved. No part of this publication may be reproduced, stored or transmitted in any form or by any means, electronic, mechanical, photocopying, recording, scanning, or otherwise without written permission from the publisher. It is illegal to copy this book, post it to a website, or distribute it by any other means without permission.

First edition

This book was professionally typeset on Reedsy.
Find out more at reedsy.com

Contents

1	Chapter 1: The Path Less Traveled	1
2	Chapter 2: Embracing the Silence	3
3	Chapter 3: The Inner Sanctuary	5
4	Chapter 4: The Dance of Resilience	6
5	Chapter 5: The Role of Nostalgia	7
6	Chapter 6: The Solitary Traveler	8
7	Chapter 7: The Power of Reflection	9
8	Chapter 8: Navigating Loneliness	10
9	Chapter 9: The Strength of Vulnerability	12
10	Chapter 10: The Creative Solitary	13
11	Chapter 11: The Wisdom of Nature	14
12	Chapter 12: The Power of Ritual	15
13	Chapter 13: The Solitary Sage	16
14	Chapter 14: The Dance of Emotions	17
15	Chapter 15: The Solitary Adventurer	18
16	Chapter 16: The Peace of Acceptance	20
17	Chapter 17: The Journey Continues	21

1

Chapter 1: The Path Less Traveled

The world is a cacophony of sounds, a kaleidoscope of sights, and a symphony of smells, each competing for our attention. Within this chaos, there are those who willingly seek the solace of solitude. They walk the path less traveled, finding peace in the quiet moments, and strength in their own company. The curious solitary is not antisocial; rather, they are introspective and reflective, finding joy in their inner worlds.

This journey into solitude is often catalyzed by life's hardships. Experiences of loss, rejection, or profound change push the solitary soul to retreat inward. In these moments of reflection, they discover an unexpected resilience. The quiet allows for introspection, and through this, they find an inner strength that propels them forward. The curious solitary learns that while the world outside can be tumultuous, the inner world can be a sanctuary of peace and resilience.

Resilience, however, is not a constant state. It fluctuates like the tides, sometimes strong and unyielding, at other times fragile and wavering. The solitary individual learns to navigate these ebbs and flows, understanding that resilience is built through experience and reflection. Each challenge faced becomes a stepping stone, building a bridge to a stronger, more resilient self.

Nostalgia often accompanies this journey. It is a bittersweet companion, a reminder of what once was and what could have been. For the solitary soul, nostalgia is not merely a longing for the past, but a source of comfort and strength. It is a way to connect with the inner self, to relive moments of joy and sorrow, and to draw strength from the memories of resilience and growth.

2

Chapter 2: Embracing the Silence

Silence can be both a friend and a foe. For the curious solitary, embracing silence is an essential part of their journey. In the absence of external noise, the mind is free to wander, to explore thoughts and ideas that might otherwise be drowned out. This quietude becomes a fertile ground for creativity and introspection, allowing the solitary individual to delve deep into their inner world.

However, embracing silence is not without its challenges. Society often views solitude with suspicion, equating it with loneliness or social dysfunction. The curious solitary must navigate these societal stigmas, learning to find peace in their own company despite external judgments. It requires a certain bravery to stand apart from the crowd, to embrace silence and solitude as valuable and enriching experiences.

In the quiet moments, the solitary soul discovers a wellspring of creativity. Without the distractions of the outside world, the mind is free to roam, to dream, and to create. Ideas flow more freely, and the solitary individual finds themselves in a state of flow, where time seems to stand still and the boundaries between the self and the creative process blur. This is where the curious solitary finds their true strength, in the ability to create and reflect in the silence.

Silence also offers a chance for introspection, for a deep and honest examination of the self. It is in these moments of quiet reflection that the solitary individual can confront their fears, their hopes, and their dreams. They can explore their innermost thoughts and feelings, gaining a deeper understanding of themselves and their place in the world. This introspection is a vital part of the journey, allowing the curious solitary to grow and evolve.

3

Chapter 3: The Inner Sanctuary

In a world that often feels overwhelming, the inner sanctuary becomes a refuge for the curious solitary. This inner sanctuary is a mental and emotional space where one can retreat from the chaos of the outside world and find peace. It is a place of comfort and solace, where the solitary individual can reconnect with themselves and their innermost thoughts.

Creating an inner sanctuary requires intentionality and effort. It involves setting aside time for solitude and reflection, and creating an environment that supports this. For some, this might mean finding a quiet corner of their home, while for others, it might involve spending time in nature. The key is to create a space where one can feel safe and at ease, free from external distractions and pressures.

Maintaining this inner sanctuary is an ongoing process. It requires regular introspection and self-care, and a commitment to prioritizing one's mental and emotional well-being. The curious solitary learns to protect their sanctuary, setting boundaries to ensure that they have the time and space they need to recharge and reflect.

In this inner sanctuary, the curious solitary can explore their thoughts and feelings without judgment or interruption. They can delve into their memories, dreams, and aspirations, gaining a deeper understanding of themselves and their place in the world. This process of introspection is not always easy, but it is essential for personal growth and self-discovery.

4

Chapter 4: The Dance of Resilience

Resilience is a dance, a delicate balance between strength and vulnerability. For the curious solitary, resilience is built through the challenges and hardships of life. Each experience of adversity becomes an opportunity to grow and develop inner strength. This dance of resilience is a continuous process, with each step forward building on the last.

The solitary individual learns to embrace both their strengths and their weaknesses. They understand that resilience is not about being invincible, but about being able to adapt and recover from setbacks. This requires a willingness to face one's fears and vulnerabilities, and to learn from them.

Reflection and introspection play a crucial role in this dance of resilience. By taking the time to reflect on their experiences, the curious solitary can gain valuable insights and lessons. They learn to recognize their own patterns of behavior and thought, and to identify the strategies that help them cope with adversity.

Building and maintaining resilience also involves self-compassion and self-care. The curious solitary learns to be gentle with themselves, to acknowledge their own needs and to prioritize their well-being. This self-compassion becomes a source of strength, allowing them to navigate the challenges of life with grace and resilience.

5

Chapter 5: The Role of Nostalgia

Nostalgia is a powerful force in the inner world of the curious solitary. It is a bridge to the past, a way to connect with memories and experiences that have shaped who they are. For the solitary individual, nostalgia is not just a longing for what once was, but a source of comfort and strength.

Nostalgia can evoke a wide range of emotions, from joy and warmth to sadness and longing. It is a bittersweet companion, reminding the solitary soul of the beauty and impermanence of life. By revisiting their memories, the curious solitary can find solace in the past, drawing strength from the moments of resilience and growth they have experienced.

However, it is important for the solitary individual to find a balance between nostalgia and living in the present. While it is natural to look back and reflect on the past, it is also essential to remain grounded in the present moment. The curious solitary learns to use nostalgia as a tool for self-reflection and growth, rather than as an escape from reality.

By embracing nostalgia in a positive way, the solitary individual can gain a deeper understanding of themselves and their journey. They learn to appreciate the richness of their experiences, and to draw strength from the memories of resilience and growth. This balance between past and present becomes a cornerstone of their inner world.

6

Chapter 6: The Solitary Traveler

Traveling alone can be a transformative experience for the curious solitary. It allows for complete immersion in new environments, unencumbered by the expectations or preferences of others. The solitary traveler moves at their own pace, exploring the world on their terms and savoring the freedom that comes with solitude.

The journey of the solitary traveler is marked by moments of profound introspection and discovery. With each new destination, they encounter different cultures, landscapes, and ways of life. These experiences broaden their perspective and deepen their understanding of the world and themselves. Traveling alone provides an opportunity to step outside the comfort zone, to confront challenges and embrace the unknown.

However, solo travel is not without its challenges. It requires a certain level of self-reliance and resilience. The solitary traveler must navigate unfamiliar places, sometimes facing language barriers and cultural differences. But these challenges are also opportunities for growth, building confidence and adaptability.

In the quiet moments of solitude, whether sitting by a serene lake or wandering through a bustling market, the solitary traveler finds a deeper connection with their inner self. The journey becomes not just an exploration of the outer world, but a journey inward, discovering new facets of their own identity and resilience.

Chapter 7: The Power of Reflection

Reflection is a powerful tool for personal growth and self-discovery. For the curious solitary, it is an essential part of their journey. Reflection allows for a deeper understanding of one's experiences, emotions, and thoughts. It provides clarity and insight, helping to make sense of the complexities of life.

The process of reflection involves taking a step back from the busyness of life, creating space for introspection. It can be as simple as journaling, meditating, or taking a quiet walk. The key is to create an environment that supports thoughtful contemplation, free from distractions and interruptions.

Through reflection, the curious solitary gains valuable insights into their own behavior and thought patterns. They can identify what brings them joy, what challenges they face, and what changes they need to make. This self-awareness is crucial for personal growth, allowing for intentional and meaningful changes in one's life.

Reflection also helps to cultivate resilience. By examining past experiences, the solitary individual can learn from their mistakes and successes. They can identify the strategies that helped them navigate challenges and build on these strengths. Reflection becomes a way to reinforce resilience, preparing the curious solitary for future challenges.

8

Chapter 8: Navigating Loneliness

Loneliness is a natural part of the solitary journey. Even the most introspective and reflective individuals can experience moments of loneliness. It is important to recognize and address these feelings, rather than ignoring or suppressing them. For the curious solitary, navigating loneliness involves understanding its root causes and finding ways to connect with others and with oneself.

Loneliness can stem from a variety of sources, such as a lack of meaningful connections, major life changes, or simply the natural ebb and flow of emotions. It is important to acknowledge these feelings and to understand that they are a normal part of the human experience. The curious solitary learns to embrace these moments of loneliness as opportunities for growth and self-discovery.

Finding ways to connect with others, even in small ways, can help alleviate feelings of loneliness. This might involve reaching out to friends and family, joining a community group, or engaging in activities that bring joy and fulfillment. The key is to find meaningful connections that resonate with one's values and interests.

Additionally, the curious solitary learns to cultivate a deep connection with themselves. This involves self-compassion, self-care, and finding activities that nourish the soul. By embracing their own company and finding joy in solitude, the solitary individual can navigate moments of loneliness with

CHAPTER 8: NAVIGATING LONELINESS

grace and resilience.

9

Chapter 9: The Strength of Vulnerability

Vulnerability is often seen as a weakness, but for the curious solitary, it is a source of immense strength. Embracing vulnerability means acknowledging one's fears, uncertainties, and insecurities. It means being open to experiencing the full range of human emotions, without judgment or suppression.

For the solitary individual, vulnerability is a path to deeper self-awareness and growth. By confronting their vulnerabilities, they learn to accept themselves fully, with all their strengths and weaknesses. This self-acceptance becomes a foundation for resilience, allowing them to navigate life's challenges with courage and authenticity.

Embracing vulnerability also involves being open to connection with others. It means allowing oneself to be seen and understood, even at the risk of rejection or judgment. The curious solitary learns to balance their need for solitude with the desire for meaningful connections, finding strength in both independence and interdependence.

In moments of vulnerability, the solitary individual discovers their true strength. They learn that it is okay to ask for help, to lean on others, and to show their true selves. This openness fosters deeper connections and a sense of belonging, enriching their inner world and strengthening their resilience.

10

Chapter 10: The Creative Solitary

Creativity is a vital aspect of the curious solitary's inner world. In the quiet moments of solitude, the mind is free to explore new ideas, to dream, and to create. The creative solitary finds joy and fulfillment in the act of creation, whether it is through art, writing, music, or other forms of expression.

Solitude provides the space and time needed for creativity to flourish. Without the distractions of the outside world, the solitary individual can immerse themselves in their creative pursuits, finding a sense of flow and fulfillment. This creative process becomes a source of joy and resilience, providing an outlet for self-expression and introspection.

However, creativity also requires discipline and dedication. The curious solitary learns to cultivate their creative practice, setting aside time for regular creative activities. They understand that creativity is not just about inspiration, but also about persistence and effort. By committing to their creative practice, they build a sense of purpose and fulfillment.

The creative solitary also learns to embrace imperfection. They understand that creativity is a process, and that not every creation will be perfect or successful. This acceptance of imperfection allows for greater freedom and experimentation, fostering a deeper connection with their creative selves.

11

Chapter 11: The Wisdom of Nature

Nature has always been a source of inspiration and solace for the curious solitary. In the presence of nature, the solitary individual finds a sense of peace and connection with the world around them. The natural world becomes a sanctuary, a place of reflection and renewal.

Spending time in nature allows for a deeper connection with the inner self. The sights, sounds, and smells of the natural world provide a rich sensory experience, grounding the solitary individual in the present moment. This connection with nature becomes a source of strength and resilience, providing a sense of calm and perspective.

The wisdom of nature also offers valuable lessons for the curious solitary. Observing the cycles of growth and decay, the changing seasons, and the resilience of the natural world provides insights into the human experience. The solitary individual learns to embrace the ebb and flow of life, finding comfort in the natural rhythms and patterns.

Nature also provides a space for introspection and creativity. Whether it is through hiking, gardening, or simply sitting by a river, the solitary individual finds inspiration and clarity in the natural world. This connection with nature becomes an integral part of their inner journey, enriching their inner world and fostering resilience.

12

Chapter 12: The Power of Ritual

Rituals provide a sense of structure and stability in the curious solitary's life. These practices, whether daily or seasonal, offer moments of mindfulness and intention. For the solitary individual, rituals become a way to ground themselves, to create a sense of continuity and purpose.

Rituals can take many forms, from simple daily routines to more elaborate ceremonies. For some, it might involve a morning meditation or a nightly journaling practice. For others, it might include seasonal celebrations or personal ceremonies that hold special meaning. The key is to create rituals that resonate with one's values and bring a sense of peace and fulfillment.

The curious solitary learns to integrate these rituals into their daily life, finding comfort and stability in the repetition. These practices become a way to connect with the present moment, to honor one's journey, and to cultivate a sense of gratitude and mindfulness. Rituals provide a sense of continuity, grounding the solitary individual in their inner world.

In times of change or uncertainty, rituals offer a sense of stability and resilience. They become a way to navigate the ebbs and flows of life, providing a sense of comfort and familiarity. For the curious solitary, rituals are not just routines, but meaningful practices that enrich their inner journey and foster a sense of resilience.

13

Chapter 13: The Solitary Sage

Wisdom is often born from solitude and introspection. The solitary sage is someone who has spent time reflecting on their experiences, gaining insights and understanding from their journey. For the curious solitary, wisdom is not just about knowledge, but about a deeper understanding of themselves and the world around them.

The journey to wisdom involves embracing both the joys and challenges of life. The solitary individual learns to see each experience as an opportunity for growth and learning. They understand that wisdom is not a destination, but a continuous process of self-discovery and reflection.

The solitary sage learns to trust their inner voice, to listen to their intuition and to honor their own insights. This self-trust becomes a source of strength, allowing them to navigate life's complexities with confidence and grace. They understand that true wisdom comes from within, and that it is cultivated through introspection and reflection.

In their interactions with others, the solitary sage offers a sense of calm and understanding. They are able to listen deeply, to offer insights without judgment, and to provide guidance with compassion. The curious solitary learns that wisdom is not just about seeking answers, but about asking the right questions and embracing the journey of discovery.

14

Chapter 14: The Dance of Emotions

Emotions are a fundamental part of the human experience, and for the curious solitary, they are a vital aspect of their inner world. The dance of emotions involves acknowledging and embracing the full range of feelings, from joy and love to sadness and fear. For the solitary individual, this dance is a path to deeper self-awareness and resilience.

The curious solitary learns to observe their emotions without judgment, to recognize them as valuable signals from their inner self. They understand that emotions are not something to be suppressed or ignored, but to be explored and understood. This emotional awareness becomes a source of strength, allowing them to navigate life's ups and downs with grace and resilience.

By embracing their emotions, the solitary individual learns to cultivate emotional intelligence. They become more attuned to their own feelings and the feelings of others, fostering deeper connections and understanding. This emotional intelligence is a vital aspect of their inner journey, enriching their relationships and their sense of self.

The dance of emotions also involves finding healthy ways to express and process feelings. For the curious solitary, this might involve creative outlets, such as art, writing, or music, or practices like mindfulness and meditation. By honoring and expressing their emotions, the solitary individual finds a sense of balance and fulfillment in their inner world.

15

Chapter 15: The Solitary Adventurer

Adventure is not just about physical exploration; it is also about exploring the unknown within oneself. The solitary adventurer seeks out new experiences and challenges, both in the outer world and within their inner world. For the curious solitary, adventure becomes a path to self-discovery and growth.

The solitary adventurer learns to embrace uncertainty and to find joy in the journey. They understand that true adventure lies not just in reaching a destination, but in the experiences and lessons learned along the way. This willingness to step into the unknown builds resilience and confidence, allowing the solitary individual to navigate life's challenges with grace and courage.

In their adventures, the solitary individual finds moments of profound connection with the world around them. Whether it is hiking through a mountain range, exploring a new city, or simply trying a new hobby, these experiences become opportunities for growth and reflection. The solitary adventurer learns to savor these moments, finding joy and fulfillment in the journey.

Adventure also involves embracing the unknown within oneself. The curious solitary learns to explore their own thoughts, fears, and dreams with curiosity and openness. This inner exploration becomes a path to deeper self-awareness and understanding, enriching their inner world and fostering

CHAPTER 15: THE SOLITARY ADVENTURER

resilience.

16

Chapter 16: The Peace of Acceptance

Acceptance is a powerful force in the journey of the curious solitary. It involves acknowledging and embracing the reality of one's experiences, without judgment or resistance. For the solitary individual, acceptance becomes a source of peace and resilience, allowing them to navigate life's complexities with grace.

The curious solitary learns to accept themselves fully, with all their strengths and weaknesses. This self-acceptance becomes a foundation for personal growth and self-discovery. By embracing their true selves, the solitary individual finds a sense of peace and fulfillment, free from the pressures of external expectations.

Acceptance also involves embracing the present moment. The solitary individual learns to find beauty and meaning in the here and now, without dwelling on the past or worrying about the future. This mindfulness becomes a source of strength, grounding the curious solitary in their inner world.

In moments of acceptance, the solitary individual finds a sense of calm and clarity. They learn to navigate life's challenges with grace, understanding that acceptance is not about giving up, but about finding peace within oneself. This acceptance becomes a cornerstone of their inner journey, fostering resilience and inner strength.

17

Chapter 17: The Journey Continues

The journey of the curious solitary is never truly complete. It is a continuous process of self-discovery, growth, and reflection. With each new experience, the solitary individual gains deeper insights into themselves and the world around them. They learn to embrace the ebb and flow of life, finding strength and resilience in their inner world.

As the journey continues, the curious solitary learns to balance solitude with connection, vulnerability with strength, and reflection with action. They understand that life is a dance of contrasts, and that true fulfillment comes from embracing the full spectrum of human experience.

The curious solitary also learns to find joy in the journey itself, rather than just the destination. They savor the moments of introspection, creativity, and connection, finding meaning and purpose in their inner world. This journey becomes a source of joy and fulfillment, enriching their life in profound ways.

In the end, "The Curious Solitary: How Resilience and Nostalgia Shape Our Inner Worlds" is a celebration of the inner journey. It is an invitation to embrace solitude, to cultivate resilience, and to find strength and joy within oneself. Through the lens of the curious solitary, we discover that the true adventure lies within, and that the journey of self-discovery is one of the most rewarding paths we can take.

In a world filled with constant noise and activity, **"The Curious Solitary: How Resilience and Nostalgia Shape Our Inner Worlds"** takes readers on a transformative journey into the rich and intricate landscapes of solitude. This book delves into the profound power of solitude, exploring how moments of quiet introspection and reflection can lead to personal growth, resilience, and a deeper understanding of oneself.

Through the lens of the curious solitary, we uncover the beauty and challenges of walking the path less traveled. The book explores the delicate balance between resilience and vulnerability, showing how life's hardships can become opportunities for growth. It delves into the role of nostalgia, not just as a longing for the past, but as a source of comfort and strength that shapes our inner worlds.

Each chapter invites readers to journey deeper into their inner sanctuary, uncovering the wisdom, creativity, and emotional richness that solitude offers. From embracing silence and building resilience, to navigating loneliness and finding peace in acceptance, this book is a celebration of the inner journey.

"The Curious Solitary" offers practical strategies for embracing solitude, fostering resilience, and finding joy in one's own company. It is a guide for those who seek to understand themselves more deeply, to find peace in their own company, and to cultivate a rich and fulfilling inner life. Through stories, reflections, and practical wisdom, this book invites readers to embrace the beauty of solitude and discover the strength and joy that come from within.

www.ingramcontent.com/pod-product-compliance
Lightning Source LLC
LaVergne TN
LVHW010445070526
838199LV00066B/6211